Original title:
Lemonade Love

Copyright © 2025 Creative Arts Management OÜ
All rights reserved.

Author: Lila Davenport
ISBN HARDBACK: 978-1-80586-341-0
ISBN PAPERBACK: 978-1-80586-813-2

The Essence of You and Me

In the kitchen, a splash of zest,
You and I, we're at our best.
Mixing joy with a dash of cheer,
Sipping shades of summer here.

With each swirl, a funny face,
Caught in sweet, tart embrace.
Stirring giggles, bright delight,
Making memories, day and night.

Chasing Summer Flavors

Sunshine in a frosty glass,
Chasing joy, we let it pass.
Lemon smiles and limey winks,
Twisting tongues, we laugh and think.

Ice cubes clink, a playful dance,
In this thirst, we take a chance.
Every sip, a flavored jest,
In bursts of citrus, we feel blessed.

Whispered Secrets in Citrus

Whispers sweet in a citrus grove,
Sharing laughs, so light we strove.
Squeezing out the day's delight,
Sticky fingers, hearts so bright.

With a twist and a zing so bold,
Every story waiting to be told.
Our laughter mixed with tangy cheer,
Together here, we've got no fear.

Sip by Sip

Pouring dreams into a cup,
Sip by sip we drink it up.
Frothy bubbles, giggles chase,
Witty chats in a sunny space.

When life hands us citrus spins,
We raise our cups, let the fun begin.
With every laugh and every cheer,
We savor moments, crystal clear.

Sunkissed Sips

In a pitcher so bright, oh what a sight,
Chilled and inviting, oh pure delight.
Mango may tease, but lemons won't quit,
With each zesty sip, we giggle and sit.

Sunshine in glasses, we clink with glee,
A squeeze of good times, just you and me.
Citrus explosions, such tangy cheer,
Enjoying this nectar, we laugh without fear.

Citrus Serenade

Under the sun, with laughter galore,
We share stories, who could ask for more?
In sweet citrus whispers, our plans interlace,
We dance with the flavors, in this happy space.

Zesty adventures, we sip and we spin,
With juicy surprises, let the fun begin.
A fruity enchantment, all troubles on pause,
Together we savor, love's merry applause.

Sweet Tang of Togetherness

With every drop, our spirits align,
Sweet and sour, it's all so divine.
We giggle and sip, the world feels just right,
In this tangy moment, we shine oh so bright.

Our toasts are filled with a slice of pure cheer,
Got laughter and love, nothing to fear.
Orange and lemon, a playful embrace,
In joyful concoctions, we find our place.

Pucker Up for Passion

With puckered lips, we laugh through the day,
A splash of delight in a fun, zesty way.
Each laugh is a bubble, each sip is a cheer,
In this tangy romance, we have no fear.

In sweet little moments, our hearts intertwine,
With every fresh sip, we're feeling just fine.
Two playful souls in citrusy bliss,
A toast to the times that we wouldn't miss.

Flavor of the Heart

In a glass so bright and clear,
Mixing giggles with a cheer.
Sour notes with laughter blend,
A silly twist, my fondest friend.

Stirring dreams with ice so chill,
Each sip just makes my heart thrill.
Citrus kisses on the tongue,
Life's a song that's still unsung.

Charmed by Citrus

Oh, those zesty vibes in spring,
Tickles heartstrings, makes us swing.
Squeezed with love, a funny flair,
In every bubble, joy to share.

A splash of giggles, so divine,
You toast the day, I sip the shine.
Sunshine spills from every drop,
With citrus zest, we never stop.

Tasting the Sweetness of Us

Straw hats tilted, we arcade roam,
Laughter melting like ice-cream cone.
Every taste, a vibrant play,
Swirling colors, come what may.

Sweetened moments, wild and free,
A hint of spice, just you and me.
Zesty smiles in every swirl,
We twirl together, boy and girl.

Savoring Sunlit Days

In the park where shadows dance,
We toast to life with a silly glance.
With every sip, a hearty cheer,
Let's sip on joy, my dear!

Suffering frowns? Just take a drink,
Citrus spark ignites the blink.
Sunlit days of laughter bright,
In every drop, there's pure delight.

A Splash of Joy

In a cup of yellow cheer,
Giggling bubbles rise high,
Sipping dreams without a care,
Winking at the summer sky.

When life gives you sour days,
Add a twist, make it shine,
With a splash of quirky ways,
Laughter's the best design.

Sweet Sunshine and Cherry Blossoms

Under trees with pink delight,
We dance with citrus glee,
Swirling flavors in our flight,
    A zesty jubilee.

Giggles pop like candy rain,
As the sun begins to gleam,
Who knew sweetness hid the pain?
    Life's a sparkling dream.

Memories on Ice

Chillin' on a sunny day,
Smiles drip from melting ice,
Tangled up in goofy play,
Life feels oh so nice.

With every sip, a memory,
Slushy flavors swirl and mix,
What a wild, zany spree,
Magic in our funny tricks.

Sipping Happiness

Pour a cup of giggles shy,
Add a splash of bubbly fun,
Underneath the cotton sky,
We chase the setting sun.

Every gulp a chuckle fine,
Bitter days are far away,
In the swirl of liquid sunshine,
We laugh while we sip and sway.

Heartfelt Refreshment

When life gives you citrus cheer,
Grab a glass, let's draw near.
With sweet and sour laughs abound,
We'll sip our joy, happiness found.

In sunlit days, we twist and twirl,
Our giggles dance, our spirits whirl.
With splashes bright, our spirits soar,
A taste of fun, we can't ignore.

Parched Souls Entwined

Two thirsty hearts on a summer spree,
Quenching thirst with glee and glee.
With each cold sip, we toast the day,
Our playful banter lights the way.

In this sweet brew, our worries drown,
Cheers to us, the joyful crown.
With straw in hand, we share the routes,
Our laughter echoes, with sips and shouts.

Flavorful Togetherness

In a picnic basket, we hide our stash,
Citrus crush that makes us splash.
Sipping stories in the sun,
With puns and jokes, it's all just fun.

We mix and mingle, concocting delight,
With tangy giggles, we feel just right.
No bitter moments would dare to stay,
When flavors blend, we laugh and play.

Summer Tastes

A twist of joy in every gulp,
Under the sky, we dance and pulse.
With zesty smiles and playful glances,
In our sunny dance, the heart enhances.

Each drop a joy, each sip a tease,
With quirks and laughs, we sail the seas.
Together we relish this silly spree,
In our vibrant cup, we find the key.

Spritz of Love

In the summer heat, we share a drink,
Sipping sweet memories, don't you think?
With a twist of zest, we giggle and sigh,
Fizzy laughs bubble up, oh me, oh my!

A splash of joy in every sip we take,
Each citrus kiss, a delightful quake.
Chasing clouds away with each sunny glance,
Pouring out happiness, come join the dance!

Magic in a Glass

Stirring up trouble with a dash of fun,
This fruity potion has just begun.
With every slosh, my heart does prance,
Ready for a sip, let's take a chance!

A swirl of color, sparkle bright,
In this shimmering glass, everything feels right.
It's silly, it's sweet, it's a recipe rare,
A toast to the moments we choose to share!

The Heart's Chilled Desire

Oh, the chill that runs down my spine,
Like icy sweetness that feels divine.
Your laughter's the straw that stirs my soul,
In this cool delight, I feel whole!

A dribble of nectar, a splash of cheer,
Mixing up smiles, nothing to fear.
Flavors collide, a funny blend,
Your glance, my zest, set hearts to trend!

Sunny Days

Under the sun, we sip with glee,
With a bit of sour that sets us free.
Your goofy grin, my favorite taste,
In this sweet sundae, let's not waste!

Bright yellow moments like rays of light,
Quirky dreams make everything right.
In every sip, a burst of delight,
Let's praise the silliness with all our might!

Sweeter Ways

Twisting those lemons, making them smile,
In our little world, we linger a while.
Mixing up giggles with every pour,
This fun concoction, who could ask for more?

Beneath the stars, our laughter rings clear,
Sipping and sharing, united in cheer.
With every laugh, we toast to the night,
Creating our magic, feeling just right!

Slices of Joy

In the sun, we squeeze and play,
With citrus smiles that light the day.
Laughter bubbles in each sip,
Sweet-tart kisses, an endless trip.

Giggles drift on summer's breeze,
We toast to charm, just as we please.
Giddy moments, bright and bold,
In every glass, a story told.

Radiant Revelry

With frothy whispers in our cups,
We dance around, while joy erupts.
Zesty jokes, a playful fling,
As tartness makes us wildly sing.

Underneath a lemon tree,
We share our dreams, it's pure esprit.
Serenade of sugar's grace,
In each other's smiles, we find our place.

Tasting Eternity

Sip by sip, we chase the sun,
With laughter's zest, we're never done.
Citrus drops like sunshine rain,
In every taste, we feel the gain.

Bubbles tickle, joy ignites,
We toast to silly, wild delights.
Time stands still, we laugh and sway,
In this moment, bright and gay.

Citrusy Connections

Frothy drinks with straw in hand,
We giggle, splash, and make a stand.
Tangy tales shared under glow,
As summer blooms, our spirits grow.

With every sip, a laughter spins,
The joy of life in all its wins.
Our hearts entwined by sunshine's cue,
In vibrant shades of yellow hue.

Frosty Moments with You

We mix the smiles and giggles,
In pitchers full of cheer,
Your laughter is my secret,
That sweetens all the year.

With every splash of citrus,
We dance around the sink,
The frosty glass a canvas,
For all the dreams we ink.

A twist of zest, a wink so bright,
We toast to silly sights,
Unruly straws and tasty sips,
Are how we spend our nights.

So let's create our magic,
In bubbly, bright display,
For every frosty moment,
Is love in a quirky way.

Sunny Elixirs

Under the sun, we ponder,
What mixes up our fun,
A dash of playful banter,
And we're the perfect one.

The joy is in our flavors,
Nectar from the sky,
With every sip we share,
We giggle, laugh, and sigh.

A splash of wild ideas,
And garnished with a grin,
We savor every moment,
And let the silliness begin.

So raise your glass, my dear,
To these elixirs bright,
In the sunshine, let's embrace,
Our cheerful, silly flight.

Embracing the Flavor

There's magic in the mixing,
A concoction for our soul,
With every quirky blend we make,
We taste the joy, make whole.

A pinch of playful chaos,
A swirl of bright delight,
Our cups runneth over,
With laughter taking flight.

We'll sip the sweetest moments,
From vessels crystal clear,
And with each zesty sip we share,
The world will feel more near.

So let's embrace each flavor,
As we steal a cheeky kiss,
In this blend of silly moments,
We find our truest bliss.

Citrus Days and Starry Nights

In a world so tart yet sweet,
We squeeze joy with our feet.
Laughter bubbles, sunshine beams,
Dancing through our citrus dreams.

With every sip, a giggle bursts,
A twist of fate, a laugh that thirsts.
Under stars, we bottle cheer,
With fruity sparkles, we draw near.

Blissful Concoctions

Mixing giggles in a jar,
Sipping sunshine from afar.
A dash of zest, a twist so bright,
Stirring joy into the night.

With every swirl, a chuckle flows,
A bubbly dance as laughter grows.
In every glass, a silly grin,
Cheers to the fun that lies within.

Bubbles of Affection

Bubbles pop like laughter's tune,
A frothy heart beneath the moon.
We sip our whims, our spirits soar,
Sharing secrets, wanting more.

Each drop of joy, a silly joke,
A tickling fizz, the best bespoke.
In kisses sweet, our truths unwind,
A playful love that's one of a kind.

Sparkling Memories

With sparkly sips, we toast our past,
Each moment fizzy, meant to last.
From goofy grins to shared delight,
We toast our dreams with all our might.

In our cups, the laughter swirls,
A tapestry of twirls and whirls.
Remember when, we giggled loud?
Our memories are joyfully proud.

The Citrus Connection

In a glass so bright and yellow,
Two hearts collide, oh what a fellow!
Gulping laughter, sweet and tangy,
Two silly straws, feeling quite fancy.

Sipping dreams beneath the sun,
Making silly faces, oh what fun!
With every gulp, we're in a trance,
Twisting, turning, in a dance.

Sunshine in Every Sip

A splash of joy, a zesty kick,
Each sip a giggle, oh so quick!
Bubbles fizzing like our laughter,
In this drink, there's a sweet disaster.

Citrus smiles on a summer day,
Sunshine sparkles in our playful way.
With each chuckle, we spill and tease,
What's a slip, if not a breeze?

Warming Hearts

Two cups clink as we chime and cheer,
Sharing secrets only we can hear.
Sticky fingers from the sweets,
In every drip, our love repeats.

Fun spills over like the fizzy drink,
Each sip reminds us what we think.
Just a little sugar, a tad of salt,
Warming hearts, never at fault.

Chilling Tastebuds

Ice cubes floating like our dreams,
With every sip, the laughter beams.
Sour and sweet, it's a mix divine,
Pucker up, let's intertwine!

Chilled delight in every pour,
Making memories is what we're for.
We toast to mishaps and silly fables,
In this zesty world, we're more than able.

A Toast to Togetherness

Raise your glass, here's to the fun,
With zesty sips, the day is won!
Every ounce is packed with cheer,
Side by side, we're so sincere.

Laughter bubbles like the drink,
With every clink, our hearts sync.
A playful spark, bright and bold,
In this citrus world, love unfolds.

Sunshine in a Jar

A jar of sunshine, just a sip,
Brings vibrant smiles and a little zip.
With sugary sweetness, we start to giggle,
For every twist, we dance and wiggle.

A splash of zest, a twist of fate,
We share our sips, can't hesitate.
Our laughter bubbles like fizz in cheer,
In this joyful drink, we have no fear.

The Zest of Us

Two citrus slices on the rim,
In our minds, we start to swim.
Sipping slowly, we share our tales,
In this quirky mix, our love prevails.

With every gulp, our spirits rise,
We trade sweet secrets, fun surprise.
Giggling soft, with a dash of sass,
This fruity potion, a playful glass.

Citrus Breeze

A breeze of citrus, warm and light,
We laugh and chat into the night.
With vibrant colors, our hearts ignite,
In silly moments, everything feels right.

With every zesty flavor shared,
We toast to fun, no moment spared.
This tangy drink, our secret code,
In laughter's flow, our spirits explode.

Refreshing Reflections

In mirrored jars, we find our glow,
With icy twists, we take it slow.
Each laugh reflects a twist of fate,
In this sunny mix, we levitate.

We sip and spill our dreams like juice,
In every giggle, we set them loose.
With sassy straws and winks to spare,
Our refreshing bond is beyond compare.

Zesty Hearts Collide

In a twist of fate, we met at noon,
Sipping chilled drinks, under the moon.
You spilled yours first, oh what a mess,
We laughed so hard, in our sticky dress.

With citrus smiles, we danced around,
Your giggle's zing, the sweetest sound.
A splash of joy, a hint of fun,
Two zesty hearts, beating as one.

Tangy Embrace

You tossed a slice, it landed near,
My heart did flip, oh dear, oh dear!
We sought the shade, just to conspire,
Chasing the sun, like kids on fire.

Our laughter mixed with fruity cheer,
Each sharp remark, more sweet, my dear.
A playful fight with straws in hand,
In this silliness, we took our stand.

Sun-Kissed Affection

Under the sky, so bright and bold,
We shared our secrets, laughter untold.
A taste so sweet, in every sip,
With every grin, we let love rip.

Your playful jabs, they made me glow,
Like sunlit juice in the summer's flow.
With every clink of chilled glass near,
Our quirky romance, so perfectly clear.

Refreshing Bliss

A picnic spread with sparkly drinks,
Four silly straws, as our heart winks.
The breeze played tricks, it swirled your hair,
We both just laughed, without a care.

As the sun dipped low, with a sigh so sweet,
We cherished the dusk, no more heat.
In our silly game, we found our bliss,
A sip, a laugh, just like a kiss.

Frosted Dreams

In a glass, so bright and gleam,
Chilled delights, a summer dream.
With a twist and little zest,
Tickles smiles, we feel our best.

Laughter bubbles, oh so sweet,
Sips of joy, a playful treat.
Citrus giggles dance and sway,
Brighten up our sunlit day.

Nectar of the Heart

Witty words, a splash of cheer,
Sour moments disappear.
With every sip, we share our tease,
Bubbles rise, we laugh with ease.

Sticky fingers, stolen sips,
Sip by sip, our laughter flips.
A tart romance in every taste,
No time wasted, no sip to waste.

A Taste of Togetherness

In a jug, we pour our tune,
Sunkissed sun and silver moon.
Stirring up our secret rhyme,
Every sip's a joyful chime.

Shared between the grins we trade,
Whimsical blend, no need to fade.
Add a dash of quirky nights,
Toasting dreams and silly flights.

Sweet Sips of Desire

Frothy crowns upon our heads,
Lemon whims and laughter spreads.
Each slurp sends a giggle cascade,
Tart and sweet, the world parades.

With a wink, we shake it right,
Fizzy moods take off in flight.
Flavors twist in cheeky ways,
In this dance, our love still plays.

Bright Days, Brighter Hearts

Sipping sunshine in a cup,
Laughing loud, we lift it up.
Every sip, a giggle shared,
Two goofy friends, perfectly paired.

Straw hats on, we dance around,
Drips of joy where love is found.
Sticky fingers, sweet on lips,
A splash of fun on summer trips.

The Vibrance of Togetherness

Twists and turns with every drink,
You tell a joke, and then I wink.
Pinky promises with zest,
In this mix, we are the best.

Bright colors swirl like our delight,
Sipping slow into the night.
A twist of fate with every sip,
Bursting laughter, friendship's trip.

Juicy Promises

In a glass, our dreams collide,
Sweetness flows, no need to hide.
Every taste, a secret told,
In this joy, we boldly mold.

Bubbles dance, a fizzy cheer,
Here's to us, bring on the year!
With each gulp, we reminisce,
Moments golden, pure bliss.

Radiance in a Glass

Pour it bright, like giggles loud,
In this cup, we're far from cowed.
Citrus dreams, a silly splash,
We chase fun, oh what a bash!

With every sip, we paint the town,
Laughs and cheers, never a frown.
Shaking hands with tangy zest,
Together, we are truly blessed.

Over Ice

Sipping joy from glass so bright,
A twist of joy, pure delight.
Rimmed with sugar, taste so grand,
Laughter bubbles, hand in hand.

In this drink, a splash of cheer,
Chilled and zesty, love is near.
On the rocks, our hearts collide,
Every sip, we take in stride.

With every slurp, giggles erupt,
Fruity fun, we can't disrupt.
Lemon twist and ice unite,
Under sunshine, all feels right.

Under Stars

Under the sky, where dreams reside,
In a cup, we take a ride.
Stars above with citrus glow,
Each sip whispers, take it slow.

The moonlight dances, our hearts race,
Frothy laughter, a sweet embrace.
A sprinkle of juice, a drop of glee,
With funny faces, just you and me.

Trading stories with every gulp,
Silly jokes, an endless yelp.
As night wraps tight, we toast and sway,
With every sip, we laugh and play.

Sunlit Sweetness

Sunshine drips with vibrant cheer,
In the glass, there's love so clear.
Zesty rays, we dance about,
Swirling flavors make us shout.

Giggling kids, a tart surprise,
Citrus magic fills the skies.
With every pour, a smile's born,
Jokes and laughter, never worn.

Golden drops feel like a joke,
Fizzy bubbles, laughter spoke.
Under the sun, we sip and sway,
In this sweetness, we'll forever stay.

Citrus Bloom

In a garden, colors bloom,
Fruits that dance, dispel all gloom.
Squeeze of joy, a vibrant hue,
Sipping, laughing, just us two.

Petals swirl, we take a seat,
Citrus laughter, oh so sweet.
With every burst, we find our way,
Giggling softly, every day.

In every sip, a grin we find,
A quirky note, a twist combined.
Golden drops of joy untold,
In this garden, love unfolds.

Our Tangy Journey

With a jar, we start to blend,
Fruity fun, let's not pretend.
Squeezed and stirred, what a delight,
On this ride, we laugh all night.

Tart and sweet on every turn,
In each moment, we shall learn.
Sunshine pouring, smiles abound,
In our hearts, joy is found.

Together we sip, together we jest,
Through every twist, we're truly blessed.
A tangy journey, hand in hand,
With every taste, we make a stand.

Loving Infusion

In the sun's bright embrace,
We sip with a happy face.
Fizzy bubbles dance along,
Our laughter sings a cheery song.

Sour notes blend with sweet,
A quirky taste, oh what a treat.
With every sip, we smile wide,
On this zestful joyride.

Citrus spin in the air,
A whimsical, tasty affair.
Your grin makes my heart race,
Like a splash of joy in a glassy space.

Let's twirl in a citrus whirl,
With flavors that happily unfurl.
In this vibrant, joyous brew,
I find my sweetest happiness with you.

Glasses Raised to Us

Clinking glasses, what's the scoop?
Bright flavors in our happy group.
Each sip tells a funny tale,
Like a euphoric citrus gale.

In this giggly, bright delight,
With fizzy fun, we take flight.
Your jokes are tangy, sweet, and bold,
Like a refreshing drink of gold.

Sour faces turn to cheer,
With every sip, you draw me near.
In caffeine dreams, we float along,
Creating our own silly song.

So here's to us, my clever mate,
With every toast, we celebrate.
Life's a party, bursting with zest,
Your company truly is the best.

Tangy Interlude

A pause in the chaos, we attend,
Sipping sweetness with a twist to blend.
Your laughter brightens the day's grumps,
Funny faces, and silly jumps.

With each tang, a burst of cheer,
Making memories year after year.
Our quirky jokes are filled with zest,
In this flavorful, goofy quest.

Lemons dancing in our heads,
Dreams of citrus, soft warm beds.
We swirl and twirl, making fun,
Under the glow of the radiant sun.

A moment plucked from the sky,
With each giggle, we can't deny.
With a chuckle, we find our way,
In this intoxicating play.

A Burst of Happiness

From quirky thoughts, we take a sip,
A twisting dance, a playful trip.
With every gulp, joy fills the air,
A sweetened mix, nothing can compare.

Sour patches turn to sweet delights,
As we giggle into cozy nights.
Your jokes are like my drink's charm,
Making every moment disarm.

Lemon pops and playful tease,
In your gaze, I find my ease.
A twist of fun in every drop,
In this joyful dance, we can't stop.

Cheers to sprightly days to come,
Where laughter flows and beats the drum.
With a burst of sunshine bright and bold,
Our funny story's waiting to unfold.

Chilled Moments of Us

On a sunny day we met,
Sipping joy from cups we set.
Dripping smiles and silly jokes,
Our laughter danced like fizzy folks.

You spilled some on your shirt,
I laughed until it hurt.
Sticky fingers, sweet with glee,
Just you, the sun, and me.

We tossed and shared our dreams,
Bubbling up like frothy streams.
Creative twists, we mixed it well,
In our world, we cast a spell.

So let's toast to the laughter,
To the fun and happy ever after.
These chilled moments, we'll recall,
Sipping sunshine through it all.

Sweet and Sour Romance

I like you more than sugar spritz,
But sometimes you throw in the sour bits.
Your smile's a twist, yet sharp and bright,
A zesty flavor, pure delight.

We tangle like straws in the glass,
Swirling sweet thoughts that come to pass.
But when you frown, it's lemon straw,
Turning giggles into awww!

Every sip a curious blend,
Of giggles shared and trends we send.
With every taste, both sweet and tart,
You've squeezed your way into my heart.

So here's a toast, my funky friend,
May our punchlines never end.
Let's juggle flavors, twist and cheer,
This sweet and sour will always steer.

The Flavor of Connection

You laughed and pulled a funny face,
As we shared that zesty taste.
Sips of joy, with sugar free,
In our little world, just you and me.

Each bubble burst, a sweet surprise,
Twinkling jokes in sunny skies.
With clinking cups, our spirits soar,
Together we mix, forevermore.

A splash of fun, a twist of fate,
With every sip, we celebrate.
In this glass of laughter's glow,
The flavor of you, I want to know.

So here's to us, the zestful pair,
In this fizzy dream, let's always share.
Through tipsy days and giggling nights,
We'll sip away and reach new heights.

Tart Whispers

In shadows soft, the laughter's light,
Whispered tales of our delight.
With sips so tart, yet sweetly sly,
You caught my eye, oh my, oh my.

The world's a glass, how it swirls,
With every twist, my heart unfurls.
You're the lemon twist, so strong and bright,
Turned the ordinary into a funny night.

With every gulp, your jokes do flow,
A friendship feast, it steals the show.
Tart whispers in a sunny breeze,
Moments shared that put us at ease.

So let's pretend we're some great stars,
Mix our joys in funky jars.
In every sip, a tale to tell,
Tart whispers bind us very well.

Refreshment of the Soul

In a glass so bright and clear,
Sunshine giggles, drawing near.
With every sip, a zesty tease,
Brings a smile that feels like breeze.

Funny moments catch my eye,
As I watch the fly on by.
It dances near my vibrant drink,
And makes me wonder, how to think?

The citrus twist, it winks at me,
A comedy, in sweet glee.
Sour moments turn to cheer,
When love's the flavor, have no fear.

So raise a glass, let laughter bloom,
In every sip, we chase the gloom.
With silly jokes and hearty cheers,
Refreshing smiles throughout the years.

Loving in Full Bloom

In the garden, love does sprout,
With every taste, there's no doubt.
Petals bright, beneath the sun,
Sipping joy, we laugh and run.

Witty banter fills the air,
As blossoms flirt without a care.
Sticky fingers reach for fruit,
In playful chaos, love takes root.

The bees join in, a buzzing choir,
While we toast to growing higher.
Finding sweetness in each glance,
Our hearts skip in a zesty dance.

So let us linger, let us play,
In love's embrace, we'll find our way.
With smiles like blossoms in the light,
We're blooming, oh, what a delight!

Golden Nectar of Bliss

From the pitcher, it cascades,
Liquid sunshine never fades.
As we sip and laugh so loud,
In this nectar, joy be proud.

Did that lemon just wink at me?
Tart and sweet, a jubilee.
We trade jokes and toast our fate,
In this golden, loving state.

Giggling as we spill a drop,
Chasing joy, we just can't stop.
With fruit and zest and laughter too,
In this sweet mix, there's me and you.

So take a moment, be my friend,
Let's toast our hearts that never end.
With every sip, we find our bliss,
In golden nectar's joyful kiss.

Sips of Sweet Serenity

With a shimmer in the glass,
Taking sips as moments pass.
Each refreshing, icy drop,
Makes the laughter never stop.

Bright umbrella overhead,
Witty lines fill up my head.
As I taste the citrus zest,
Life's a joke; let's run the quest.

Giggling, chatting, sharing tales,
As we dodge the playful gales.
Sip by sip, our worries fade,
In this laughter, love's displayed.

So here's to joy, both near and far,
With each new sip, we raise the bar.
In sweet serenity, let it flow,
Embracing fun in every glow.

Zesty Adventures Await

In a glass so bright, a splash of cheer,
Sipping sunshine, nothing to fear.
Laughter bubbles like fizzy delight,
Chasing the blues into the night.

We twirl like fruit on a lazy spin,
Kitchen chaos where the fun begins.
Rinds are flying, zest takes flight,
Creating joy, oh what a sight!

With a wink and a grin, we stir the mix,
Painting our world with sugary tricks.
Every sip a giggle, every drop a song,
Together, my friend, we can't go wrong.

So grab a straw, let's make a toast,
To our silly hearts, we love the most.
In this party of flavors, dreams take shape,
Zesty adventures, let's escape!

Heartstrings Mixed with Sugar

Sweetness drips from every shared joke,
A blend of laughter, the perfect stroke.
We dance in the kitchen, creating a scene,
With sticky fingers, we're a sugary team.

Citrus giggles fill up the air,
Like sunshine caught in a messy hair.
Silly faces, flavors collide,
A carnival of joy we won't hide.

With each zesty twist, our hearts do sway,
Stirring up love in a playful display.
We toss in a wink and a dash of zest,
In this sweet concoction, we feel blessed.

As the sun sets, we sip side by side,
A fizzy friendship, our hearts open wide.
Together we laugh, through thick and thin,
In our sugary mix, there's always a win.

Squeeze of Sweetness

A squeeze of joy in every sip,
With giggles and grins, we happily trip.
Fruit slices dance upon the rim,
A quirky tale, where the light's never dim.

In the blender, a whirl of delight,
Stirring our dreams till they shine bright.
Chilling together, we share a blast,
Moments like these always hold fast.

A tangy twist to our silly chat,
Mixing up memories, can you beat that?
With every sip, a quirk or two,
In our world of flavor, there's always a view.

So let's keep sipping and spinning tales,
On zesty adventures, where joy prevails.
In our cup of fun, we'll always find,
A squeeze of sweetness, forever entwined.

Citrus Kisses in Summer

Under the sun, we share a grin,
Refreshing flavors pull us in.
Splashing citrus, giggles abound,
In our sweet haven, joy is found.

Brambling tales with a twist of lime,
Every moment a burst, a splash of rhyme.
We're crafting memories, sticky and sweet,
On this summer day, life feels complete.

A tilt of the glass, watch it shine,
Each sip a kiss of sunshine divine.
With every chuckle, our hearts expand,
In a playful world, hand in hand.

At dusk we clink our glasses high,
Chasing the stars in the summer sky.
Citrus delights, so bright and bold,
In laughter's embrace, our stories unfold.

A Brew of Bliss

In a jar of sunshine, joy does swirl,
With giggles and chuckles, around they'll twirl.
Sipping on sweetness, a tangy delight,
Bubbling with laughter, everything's bright.

Chasing the clouds, we dance with glee,
Mixing up flavors, just you and me.
Whisking up memories, oh what a sight,
In this zesty moment, everything's right.

Sour and sassy, but oh so fun,
Taking sweet sips, beneath the sun.
Each tangy twist brings forth a grin,
Together in chaos, let the day begin.

With a splash of sparkle, we raise our cups,
Toast to the funny, and all the hiccups.
Frothy and fizzy, let the good times roll,
In this brew of bliss, we find our soul.

Tart Kisses

A mist of citrus, bright and zesty,
With silly jokes that keep us testy.
We twirl in flavors, a lively show,
Tartness lingers, oh what a glow.

Puckering lightly with every taste,
Chasing each smile, nothing's misplaced.
Bubbles of laughter, they fill the air,
As we sip slowly, without a care.

Sweetness and tang, a playful mess,
Toasting with joy, we feel the excess.
With every giggle, our hearts entwine,
Tart kisses shared, oh how divine.

In the midst of madness, we find our fun,
Under the sky, we shine like the sun.
A jar packed with giggles, come take a sip,
With tart little kisses, let's take a trip.

Infused with Happiness

In a pitcher of smiles, we mix and spin,
Zesty concoctions, where fun begins.
Sprinkles of joy, in every swirl,
A dash of laughter, watch the bubbles unfurl.

Bright yellow sunshine, pouring a glow,
Stirring up giggles, putting on a show.
Each sip reveals, a playful surprise,
A festival of flavors, where silly lies.

Sour bursts and sweet little winks,
With every gulp, the spirit shrinks.
Infused with happiness, we toast our plight,
In this charming chaos, everything's right.

So gather the friends, let's make a cheer,
Giggles and squirts, with no hint of fear.
Here's to the nectar, that fills our days,
Infused with happiness, in zany ways.

Essence of Sweetness

In the cup of joy, our dreams collide,
Juicy adventures, where laughter won't hide.
Squeezed a bit tightly, yet so divine,
Essence of sweetness, you're truly mine.

With twirls and swirls, we spin our tale,
Tickled by flavors, we giggle and sail.
A cheeky burst, with each little zest,
In this fountain of fun, we jest with the best.

Bright lemons dancing, in a sparkling stream,
Every sip taken, feels like a dream.
With playful intentions, we sip and we slurp,
Each moment we share, a joyful little burp.

So here's to the sweetness, in every pour,
Chasing our worries, forevermore.
With sparkly eyes and joyous delight,
Essence of sweetness makes everything right.

Juicy Daydreams

On a sunny canvas, we sip our dreams,
With giggles floating in fizzy streams.
Straw hats and shades, oh what a sight,
Chasing the bubbles, hearts taking flight.

Sour twists in a sweetened embrace,
You splash lemon zest on my smiling face.
With every sip, we burst into cheer,
Lemon drops dance, my dear, oh so near.

Wuffling straws, they tickle our noses,
Like silly daffodils in funny poses.
A twist of joy in every swirl,
We're just two kids in a citrus whirl.

Under a sky that's perfectly blue,
Every drop of laughter feels wonderfully new.
As whipped cream clouds fluff the sunny hue,
In our juicy daydreams, I'm stuck like glue.

The Zing of Togetherness

With a pinch of zest and a splash of cheer,
We mix up giggles, oh dear, oh dear!
Sipping on sunshine, we sneak in a swirl,
Catching smiles like a dancing whirl.

Your laughter's the syrup that sweetens my day,
In this fizzy cocoon, we giggle and sway.
Cherries on top of our laughable spree,
Bringing the zing from you straight to me.

Stirring up mischief, we stir it just right,
Our bubbles are bursting, oh what a sight!
This slushy concoction of joy and delight,
Tastes of moments that shine so bright.

With each sunny sip, our hearts intertwine,
In this quirky world, everything's divine.
Let's raise our glasses, let's make a toast,
To the zing of togetherness we love the most.

Summer's Tender Touch

Warm rays drench us in a golden hug,
Tickling our toes like a playful bug.
Sipping on giggles from colorful cups,
Floating in laughter, never giving up.

Ice cubes clink like laughter in a jar,
You make the sun look like a falling star.
Each sip a giggle, each smile a cheer,
With flavors of joy, we chug for a year.

As the breeze whispers secrets so sweet,
We dance on the grass, feel the summer heat.
With flavors that pop, oh what a rush,
Together we blend in this summertime hush.

So here's to the rays, to the joyous crush,
In this playful season, we bubble and blush.
With every cool sip, my heart takes flight,
In summer's tender touch, the world feels right.

Heartfelt Swirl

In a frosty glass, our giggles unite,
Swirling together, our hearts feel light.
With every sip, our troubles dissolve,
In this silly potion, our smiles evolve.

Pucker and giggle, oh what a tease,
Like a wild breeze rustling through the trees.
Under the sun, we twirl and we spin,
With fruity delights bubbling deep within.

Every sip's an encore, laughter echoes wide,
In this playful moment, it's you by my side.
With flavors that giggle and tickle the tongue,
Our hearts intertwine while the world's still young.

So let's sip forever, in this circle of fun,
Chasing the bubbles until day is done.
In the sweet swirl of heartbeats so bold,
Together we conquer, a story unfolds.

Sunlit Moments in a Glass

In the sunshine, we twirl and sip,
Puckered smiles on every lip.
A splash of joy, a dash of cheer,
Sipping laughter, my dear!

The ice cubes dance in glee,
As citrus dreams float free.
With every gulp, we chase the light,
Bubbles burst and hearts take flight!

Sticky fingers, sweet delight,
We giggle till the fall of night.
Drizzled sunshine on our skin,
Let the silly games begin!

Oh, the tang of silly fun,
Every sip, a race we've run.
Refreshing moments filled with zest,
In this glass, we find our best!

Quenching Heartstrings

In a cup, our laughter brews,
Sour notes wrap 'round our views.
With a twist, we shake the blues,
Citrus crush, we can't refuse!

Tickled tongues from every squeeze,
Sweet and tangy, just like these.
With each sip, a playful spark,
Chasing shadows in the park!

Our giggles bubble, hope runs wild,
You're my partner, fun and mild.
Straws entwined in sweet embrace,
Together, we explore this space!

And when the cup runs dry and low,
We mix it up for one more show.
Here's to cheer, a silly toast,
To the flavors we love most!

The Zest of Affection

With a wink, we raise our glass,
Tart and sweet as moments pass.
Laughter's the recipe we share,
Sipping joy beyond compare.

A slice of laughter floats on top,
Giggling till our jaws do drop.
In this swirl of joy and cheer,
I'm the fruit, and you're my dear!

Pucker up for this dance of taste,
With our hearts, we'll never waste.
Squeeze the fun from every day,
Together we'll find our way!

Sugar rush and playful jests,
In this mix, we are the best.
A fizzy pop of sweet delight,
Forever our hearts take flight!

Refreshing Whispers

Underneath the sunny rays,
We share secrets in sweet plays.
Gulping giggles, hearts collide,
Sparkling glances, joy can't hide!

Stir the pot, let flavors blend,
Every sip, we twist and bend.
Whirls of laughter spill and flow,
In this brew, our feelings glow!

Zesty tales we weave with grace,
Bubbling over in this space.
With every sip, a riddle spun,
In each drop, we have our fun!

So let's refill and toast anew,
To silly dreams, just me and you.
In this drink of pure delight,
We'll dance till the stars ignite!

Golden Drops of Joy

In a jar of sunshine bright,
I found a drink, oh what a sight!
Sipping joy with every drop,
A giggle spurt, no way to stop.

Lemon twirls in sugar's dance,
Mellow sweetness, what a chance!
Bubbling laughter in my cup,
With every taste, I lift it up.

Frothy foam and silly straws,
Breaking rules, I raise my paws!
Sour bites, then sweet delight,
Golden drops, they feel so right.

So come and splash in citrus cheer,
Each sip brings the smiles near!
Let's toast to zesty afternoons,
In our quirky lemonade tunes.

Quench the Thirst

When life gives you lemons, cheer!
Pour some giggles, never fear!
A splash of joy with every swirl,
In my cup, I twirl and whirl.

Chill it down with silly ice,
Add some sparkle, oh so nice!
Mentally wise, I sip my way,
Laughing loudly, come what may!

Sour faces turn to glee,
Lemon zest, a mystery!
Quench the thirst, let's have some fun,
Life's zesty ride has just begun!

With every gulp, a funny tale,
A citrus breeze, we set the sail!
Through bubbling joy and brightened eyes,
We'll sip our way to sunny skies.

A Sip of Sunshine

With a twist, I take a sip,
Joyful bubbles on my lip!
Bright and tangy, oh what a treat,
Sour giggles dance in my feet.

In my glass, a zesty cheer,
Golden rays and giggles near!
Sipping slow, it's such a game,
Every gulp ignites the flame.

Popping flavors, oh so sweet,
Each delightful, sour beat!
Cartwheeling through a citrus spree,
One last sip, come laugh with me!

So raise your cup, let's toast tonight,
With joyous zest, we'll feel so right!
In sunny drinks, we find our way,
Through laughter's light, let's play the day.

Citrus Serenade

In the glass, a song appears,
Citrus notes to warm our cheers!
Silly straws and fruity fun,
Sipping laughter, one by one.

Beneath the sun, we dance and swirl,
With every sip, our joy unfurl!
Fizzy whispers, sweet delight,
Citrus serenade takes flight.

Sticky hands and smiles abound,
Lemon giggles all around!
Sour patches in the mix,
Giggling softly, nothing's fixed.

So let's sip a sunny song,
In this moment where we belong!
Each drop a wink, each laugh a cheer,
Citrus magic, bring it near!

Tangy Dreams and Sugared Hopes

In a world of citrus twirls,
We dance with lemon curls.
Tasting joy in every sip,
Giggles come with every drip.

Jars of sweetness line the paths,
Sour laughs and silly gaffs.
Witty chats under sunny skies,
With every splash, a new surprise.

Squeeze the day, let worries drop,
With zesty zest, we'll never stop.
Adventures bubble, fresh and bright,
Happiness shining, pure delight.

When life gets tart, we simply grin,
Dancing with our lemonade kin.
In this mix of joy and fun,
Together we shine, a radiant sun.

Squeeze of Sunshine

A twist, a turn, a joyous whirl,
Sweet nectar makes our thoughts unfurl.
With every sip, we laugh and cheer,
Sunny stories, crystal clear.

Lemons giggle upon their trees,
Special friends, just like you and me.
Citrus secrets shared with glee,
Brightening days, wild and free.

Chill it down, let good times roll,
With ice cubes dancing in the bowl.
Each drop's a smile, a cheeky toast,
To all the moments we love most.

Sip by sip, we laugh aloud,
Together we stand, a happy crowd.
With zest for life, we raise our glass,
To sweetened memories that forever last.

Bright Drops of Joy

Squeezing life to find the sweet,
Each drop of joy can't be beat.
With silly straws in bright array,
We sip our worries right away.

Laughter bubbles, dancing high,
As we mix flavors, oh my, oh my!
Adding sprinkles, a touch of fun,
Together, we're never outdone.

Chilling moments on summer days,
Zesty humor in playful ways.
Every bottle's filled with cheer,
Sharing goodness, year by year.

So pull a chair, let's take a stand,
Bright drops of joy, they're close at hand.
With every spill and every grin,
In this crazy world, let's dive in!

Sweetened Sentiments

Underneath the summer sun,
Sugar laughs, this day is fun.
Fragrant memories fill the air,
We slosh and splash without a care.

Sipping slow with friends so dear,
Creating magic, year by year.
Witty puns around the jar,
Our hearts, they radiate like a star.

Layered sweetness, tangy bold,
Every sip a story told.
With every laugh, a tale to share,
Wonder-filled moments, simply rare.

So raise your glass, give a cheer,
Embrace the joy that draws us near.
In our confections, dreams ignite,
Sweetened sentiments, hearts in flight.

Sunkissed Moments

On a sunny day, we sip with glee,
Dancing shadows in a lemon tree.
With every gulp, a giggle spills,
Sweet and sour, it gives us thrills.

Watch the fuzzy bees as they zoom,
Buzzing to our lemonade bloom.
Lemon wedges grin in the glass,
Sipping slow, we let life pass.

Sticky fingers, splashes fly,
Of citrus drops that reach the sky.
With laughter loud and puns in tow,
Our sunny zest begins to flow.

In this bright and zany land,
Every sip feels just so grand.
Charming moments, full of fun,
Sunkissed days, they weigh a ton.

Tasting the Sun

A twist of lime upon my lip,
Sipping dreams on a citrus trip.
With straws like rockets shooting high,
Each sip a laugh, oh me, oh my!

Funny faces, squinting eyes,
As bright as summer's buzzing flies.
Dripping messes, sticky hands,
In fruity fun, together we stand.

Sip by sip, we concoct our brew,
A lemonade hue in every view.
The sun above, our laughter's sound,
In taste of joy, we all are found.

Memories swirling, spin and twirl,
In this glass, our hearts unfurl.
Golden elixirs, love poured right,
Rays of joy in every bite.

The Elixir of Affection

With a pinch of zest, we start the show,
Squeeze of laughter, let feelings flow.
Bubbles tickle, swirls they make,
A sweet concoction for love's own sake.

Peel the rinds, let laughter burst,
Sour faces make sweetness thirst.
With every gulp, a loving tease,
Caught in citrus, a heart's disease.

As we sip from the quirky cup,
Sharing giggles, can't get enough!
Fizzy dreams in the summer's glow,
Every sip brings a playful flow.

Together tangled in love's embrace,
Glasses raised in zesty grace.
Our laughter's volume hits the sky,
With each sweet sip, oh me, oh my!

Charmed by the Citrus

In the shade where the lemons sway,
We concoct smiles in a bright bouquet.
Sipping magic from a jar,
Lemon tang makes us feel like stars.

With playful sips and silly faces,
We chase joy through sunny places.
Funny tales swirl in our drinks,
With every twist, my heart just blinks.

Giggling through a citrus maze,
In a splash of smiles, our laughter plays.
Sweet and tart in perfect blend,
Our summer love that knows no end.

The air is thick with sweet delight,
Charmed by citrus, all feels right.
Together we'll sip till dusk arrives,
In sparkly moments, our spirit thrives.

www.ingramcontent.com/pod-product-compliance
Lightning Source LLC
Chambersburg PA
CBHW051729290426
43661CB00122B/134